Coping Like A King

By Melodie Yarber-Rhodes

An Interactive Journal for
Black & Brown Boys

Published by
Sula Too Publishing

Copyright(c) 2021 By Melodie Yarber-Rhodes
All rights reserved. No part of this book may be reproduced in any form or by any electronic or mechanical means, including information storage and retrieval systems, without permission in writing from the publisher, except by reviewer or presenter, who may quote brief passages in a review or presentation. Recording of the work is strictly prohibited.

Published by Sula Too Publishing, Tampa, Florida
Printed in the United States of America
www.sulatoo.com/publishing

ISBN-13: 978-1-7365717-2-9

DEDICATION

This book is dedicated to God and all the beautiful black boys He created ... past, present, and future. I hope you find your voice, and I pray you find your peace.

To Micaiah and Mason, my princes and future kings. To my husband, Tarrence, you are a King. Thank you all for your inspiration in my life.

TABLE OF CONTENTS

FOR MY PARENTS & CAREGIVERS 1

A LETTER TO "MY BOYS"- REAL TALK 2

WHO ARE YOU? 3
    What Do You Like? 6
    How Do People See ME? 10
    Emotions Are a Part of YOU! 12
    What Triggers You? 15

What Else Is There? 17
    Faith 17
    Culture 19

WHO ARE YOU? 22
    How Are You Doing Today? 26
    Who Do You Talk to When 27
    What Exactly is a "King"? 31

HOW ARE YOU COPING? 33
    7 Ways to Cope 34

WHAT DO YOU NEED TO SUCCEED? 42
    Planning For Success 45
    Skills 50
    Has Anyone Ever Told You...? 53

INSPIRATION 57

CONCLUSION 59

30 DAY JOURNAL WRITING CHALLENGE 60

ABOUT THE AUTHOR 73

FOR MY PARENTS & CAREGIVERS

Do you often find that your son is quiet and does not express his feelings? Do you have a hard time finding out what is happening when you know something is wrong? Do you find that your son is angry and/or moody a lot and you don't know why? Or you know why, but can't seem to find a solution?

If so, you are not alone. This was also my struggle.

I want you to stop right now and think of the power you hold. YOU can influence the course of your son's/grandson's life by the things you do and teach him right now!

So yes, I have two black boys, one is 16 going on 30, and the other is 2 years old. I know the struggles you are facing. Since our children don't come here with instructions, raising them can be very difficult and confusing.

I wrote *Coping Like A King* to help you and your son(s). I wanted to help your growing son to become a well-adjusted, resilient person. *Coping Like A King* is designed to help address his social and emotional needs that oftentimes go unaddressed and ignored. When those needs go unaddressed or ignored, oftentimes boys will shut down or act out. Giving them a space to work through their thoughts and feelings is a great step toward their mental and emotional well-being.

Coping Like A King is a book/interactive journal that would give black boys a tool to express themselves and to be honest with how they are feeling about life and current events. Black boys face so many challenges and obstacles in daily life and hold so much in, and I didn't find ANY resources I deemed specifically for them. That was a huge problem for me.

The passages and exercises in this book are designed to help your son learn more about himself, express himself on paper through journaling and other activities, and to help him learn how to communicate better with others. This will help him become more emotionally and mentally resilient.

> *It is my prayer that this book allows guidance and healing for your young man and that it opens new opportunities for him. I also want you to talk with him about the activities and exercises he finds the most beneficial for him. The sooner they begin working in this book, the more confident and resilient they will become. God Bless!*

Melodie

"It is easier to build strong children, than to repair broken men." - Frederick Douglas

A LETTER TO "MY BOYS" - REAL TALK

Dear Young Man,

Over the years, I have been a mother to many students. I am also a mother to two young boys that I birthed. I have spent many hours thinking about how I can help improve your outlook in life, because I have had conversations with many of you who feel misunderstood, stressed, and angry.

I am here to tell you that you can have a great life, and feel happier than you have ever been.

Things can change, and things will get better.

The only thing you can control in your life is YOU. You control you and you control how you choose to react to each circumstance, day by day.

I want you to journey through these pages with expectations that you will find something that will be helpful to you for the rest of your life.

I know you have heard and seen some things that have upset you or even enraged you. Maybe at home or maybe something happening in your community. If it made you angry, that is OK. It is human nature to be angry, sad, or even feel confused sometimes. But what will you do with that ANGER?

What will you do with that sadness?

Perhaps you are not angry at all. Maybe you are fine, but you could benefit from some goal-setting skills or learning how to talk to other people. These are also things you will learn as you interact with this journal.

Whatever the case, every one of us will struggle with something throughout our life-time and it is important that we learn how to respond and adjust so that we can become successful people. You can be happy and successful, and you will overcome all the negativity in your life.

Keep going and keep striving, because today is a new day and you can begin fresh.

I hope you enjoy this book and let me know how I can make it better for the next issue.

Take care and God bless you.

Melodie

WHO ARE YOU?

*"If you have no confidence in self,
you are twice defeated in the race of life.*

*With confidence, you have won
even before you have started."*

-Marcus Garvey

Marcus Garvey was born in 1887, when the world was different. In the United States, he was a noted Civil Rights activist who founded the *Negro World* newspaper, a shipping company called Black Star Line, and the Universal Negro Improvement Association (UNIA), a fraternal organization of black nationalists. He was a leader in his community and in the world. He taught black people to be united, to know themselves, and about the value they held as individuals and as a group.

WHO ARE YOU?

Someone once told me that if you do not know who you are, you cannot know where you are going. I think this is true. What do you think?

Now that I have your attention, hopefully, you can take your Airpods, earphones, headthingys out and read a little further.

To begin, knowing yourself means knowing what you like and what you dislike. It is also knowing what you are good at and what you could improve. Some of these things are easy to figure out - like knowing the things that you like or enjoy doing. Some can be harder to figure out - like what you are good at.

Another thing that can be a little difficult is knowing how you feel and how to deal with your feelings. Responding to your feelings is part of your personality. You might know some kids who are always happy. They smile a lot and maybe have a lot of friends.

Other kids might be anxious and worry a lot. They are usually nervous or scared.
So how does knowing yourself help you? What do you like? What do you dislike?

Put your thoughts on the lines below:

Knowing myself will:

_____

_____

I like:

_____

_____

I dislike:

_____

_____

MELODIE YARBER-RHODES  COPING LIKE A KING

WHO ARE YOU?

Draw or paste a picture of yourself in the box below. If you draw, I want details. Draw your typical face. Include your eyes and mouth. What is your expression. Make it real.

ME

MELODIE YARBER-RHODES  COPING LIKE A KING

WHO ARE YOU?

What Do You Like?

You are a unique person. You are one of a kind. You were born with some genetic information that you inherited from your mom and dad. They both contributed to making you and here you are!

> **UNIQUE**
> /yoōˈnēk/
> being the only one of its kind; unlike anything else.

There are certain things you like to do and certain things you do not like to do. These are things no one teaches you to like or dislike, it kind of comes naturally.

For me, I have always liked reading and music. I like music of all types, but my favorite music genres (types) are gospel, and hip hop (weird huh?) I also like to dance, volunteer, and travel.

My oldest son has different things he enjoys. He likes playing video games, going on social media to interact with his friends, and he likes playing sports (sometimes).

So, what do YOU like? What puts a smile on YOUR face? List your top 3.

1. _____
2. _____
3. _____

It is important to know what you like. When you know what you like, you can sometimes look forward to doing those things when you are having a bad day or when you must complete something.

Knowing what you like can also be a part of some of your coping skills. Coping skills simply means the things we do to help us through hard times or stressful situations.

WHO ARE YOU?

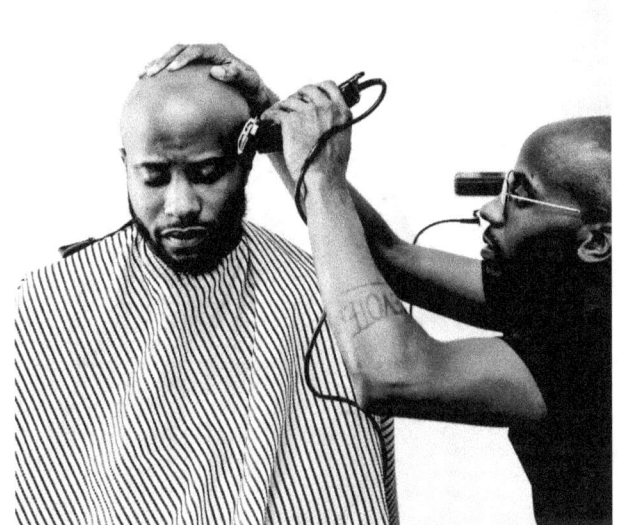

Now, let's think about things you might like, but have never tried. For whatever reason, some people will want to do things or try new fun things, but they never do! And then when they get older, they say "I wish I would have."

Are there things in your life that you want to try or participate in, but something is holding you back?

WHO ARE YOU?

WHAT DO YOU WANT TO TRY/DO?

WHAT IS HOLDING YOU BACK?

WHAT CAN YOU DO ABOUT IT?

WHO ARE YOU?

Let's go over an example:

When I was a school counselor, I worked with students of all ages and backgrounds. I had students who were shy, and I had students who were very outgoing and talkative.

I had one student who was very quiet and reserved. His teachers loved him, and he always made good grades. One day, as I was walking to lunch duty, he called for me and asked could I call him down from class because he needed to talk to me about something very important, so I told him I would try my best.

I was able to call him down later that day, and when he arrived at my office, he said he wanted some advice.

See, he was quiet and labeled as shy, but he wanted to try out for a spot in the upcoming school talent showcase. However, he had never done anything like that and didn't want to embarrass himself.

(Have you ever felt like that? I know I have!)

We talked about his talent, what he had planned in his head, and how it would look. As we talked more about details, his confidence grew.

He loved to dance, and he realized he had danced for his family members before. He got all kinds of positive praise when he did dance in front of them, so he must have been doing something good.

He eventually decided to recruit two of his friends to dance with him and they came up with a routine for tryouts. They earned a spot in the show, performed in the show, and they did their thing!

Although they didn't win any physical award, this young man gained confidence in himself by going for it and trying something new. He gained a life-long reward. He didn't let his fear hold him back, and he didn't let "what could go wrong" control him.

WHO ARE YOU?

How Do People See ME?

Another question to think about is how do you think other people see you?

Usually, by the time you reach your age, you have heard people call you certain things, like funny, mean, or cute. Perhaps you have been called intelligent or smart. Sadly, some people may be mean and say mean and negative things about you or to you, but guess what? It doesn't make it TRUE!

Throughout your life, you will meet nice people, but you will also meet MEAN people. It is important that you learn how to deal with the not so nice people in this world now, so that you can AVOID trouble. We will talk about those skills later.

"Don't Change so people will like you.

Be yourself and the right people will love the real you."
— Unknown

If you don't know how other people see you, a good way to find out is to ASK! I know it can be hard to ask people about YOU but asking is a good way to get answers.

A good tip is to ask the people who LOVE you. You can start with your family members, like mom or dad, Nana or Granddad, or your siblings. You can even ask your favorite teacher. These people care about you and will tell you how they see you and maybe even offer help if you need it.

Jot down some of the words people use to describe you. Also, I want to do a little exercise with you.

After you speak with your loved ones, you will jot down the words or sentences that people use to describe you and all your wonderful essence. Next to that, you will write if you agree with it or not AND why. Finally, you will write what you can do about it, if anything.

WHO ARE YOU?

How Do People See ME? Cont'd

What They Say?	Do I Agree/Disagree And Why?	How Does This Make Me Feel?	What Can I Do About This?

*** Sometimes it can be difficult to talk to people. If you find that you have a hard time talking to people, try writing out your question on paper and giving it to a loved one. ***

Use the space below to write out your thoughts:

_____

_____

_____

_____

_____

_____

_____

WHO ARE YOU?

Emotions Are a Part of YOU!

I know, I know, you are a boy and maybe you have heard that you are not supposed to do certain things. Raise your hand if you have been told you are NOT SUPPOSED TO CRY?!?

I hope not, but if you have, you are not alone. Too many young men have heard this message from their parents. (Don't be mad at them. They are doing the best they can. You did not come with instructions.)

Well, I am here to tell you that emotions are naturally a part of you! You can cry, and you will feel sad at different times of you life. You can feel whatever you are feeling emotionally, and it is important that you allow yourself the chance to feel those feelings.

You are a human being and having emotions is natural.

Listed below, are the top 6 emotions experienced by humans (Paul Eckman):

	HAPPY
	FEARFUL/AFRAID
	SAD
	DISGUSTED/ANNOYED
	ANGER

MELODIE YARBER-RHODES   COPING LIKE A KING

WHO ARE YOU?

Emotions Cont'd - What Are Some Things That Make You?

HAPPY

_____
_____
_____
_____
_____

FEARFUL/AFRAID

_____
_____
_____
_____
_____

SAD

_____
_____
_____
_____
_____

DISGUSTED/ ANNOYED

_____
_____
_____
_____
_____

ANGRY

_____
_____
_____
_____
_____

WHO ARE YOU?

For my artists, here is a space to draw your feelings. Do your thing.

What Other Feelings Do You Have?
_____
_____
_____

What Do You Think About Them?
_____
_____
_____

Who Do You Talk To When You Are "feeling some type of way?"
_____
_____
_____

WHO ARE YOU?

What Triggers You?

Since you have emotions, at times you will find that certain things make you react in a certain way. What do I mean by this?

Have you ever noticed that some music you listen to makes you feel happy or angry while other types of music and songs make you feel a different way?

What about noticing the music you choose to listen to at different moments of your life?

Kareem, a football player at one of my previous schools, once told me "I listen to Chief Keef before a game. He gets my head where it needs to be."

A trigger is something that affects your mood and emotions. Triggers can have positive or negative effects on you. For example, I love to travel but I do not necessarily like flying on an airplane. When I book my ticket and know that I will have to get on a plane soon, that triggers my anxiety. I think about the crowds in the airport, I worry about missing the flight, and of course, I think about how high I will be up in the air!

I have learned how to lessen this anxiety by using different strategies along the way. One thing I have learned to do is plan ahead and think about all of the things I need in order to get to the airport on time. Planning is a strategy that calms my nerves and I think less about missing the flight.

So what triggers you? I think it's important to start to look at this now so you can learn how to handle yourself and how to respond to a person, place, or thing that triggers you. On the next page, you will identify your triggers, what happens when you are triggered, and what you can do to safely respond to those triggers.

WHO ARE YOU?

Trigger	What Happens to Me? What Do I do?	How Can I Respond To It?
Example: Someone yells at me	I get angry and throw things	Instead of throwing things, I can walk away

WHO ARE YOU?

What Else Is There?

Faith

"Faith gives us hope, so if faith is lost, hope flees away like mist in the wind. Loss of faith leads to loss of hope, which leads to despair." – Dr. Myles Munroe

Dr. Myles Munroe was born in a very poor section of the island of Nassau, Bahamas. He overcame plenty of adversities such as poverty and discrimination, to become one of the most influential motivational speakers and pastors of his time. He always pointed people to his relationship with God and the power of self-discovery. Sadly, he passed away in 2014, but his work reached millions of people worldwide through books, television and all forms of media.

WHO ARE YOU?

What Else Is There? - Faith

I think that there is another part of you that is often ignored, and not talked about. Depending on your household and who you live with, you may have been exposed to some type of religion or spiritual upbringing or perhaps you have not had any exposure.

Some people find comfort in having someone to pray to and having a belief in something you view as higher than yourself.

Some people call this person God, some people call him Allah, others have other names for the person they pray to.

I think it is important to think about the spiritual side of you. It is also a part of you, in fact some people think your spiritual side is the most important part of you.

What do you think?

_____

_____

Do you have a religion or spiritual practice? If so, what is it?

_____

_____

How do you feel when you go to church, mosque, or synagogue (or another place where people gather in your religion/spiritual practices)?

_____

_____

WHO ARE YOU?

Culture

I know you have heard this word before, but do you know what it means?
What does culture mean to you?

You can draw or write a response in this box:

```
┌─────────────────────────────────────────────────┐
│                                                 │
│                                                 │
│                                                 │
│                                                 │
│                                                 │
│                                                 │
└─────────────────────────────────────────────────┘
```

Where are your parents/guardians from?
_____

_____

Where are your grandparents from?
_____

_____

What types of traditions do you celebrate or complete throughout the year?
_____

_____

WHO ARE YOU?

Culture - The African Diaspora

Did you know that there are black and brown people residing all around the world? Throughout history, black people have emigrated from Africa to travel and settle in different areas of the world. Black and brown people have been explorers for centuries, have established prosperous kingdoms and nations, and have laid the foundation for mathematics, science and other disciplines so much so that other nations came to learn from them.

As an educator, I know that in American schools, you were first introduced to Black History through the lens of slavery, however, your story did not begin there. For example, according to several historians such as Henry Louis Gates Jr., free Africans arrived in North America over a century before the transatlantic slave trade even began. There is a PBS series entitled *The Africans Americans, Many Rivers To Cross*, and I encourage you to watch it. It explains more of the history of Africans and their travels around the globe.

In addition, there are artifacts and statues with African features in places such as Mexico that indicate black people had a civilization there dating back to 1200-400 BC! These people were called the Olmecs. The discovery of statues like these changed people's understanding of black history and their travels throughout the world. In addition, an African-Mexican president abolished slavery in Mexico in 1829.

WHO ARE YOU?

There are Afro-Latinas, Afro-Cubans, Brazilians, Haitians and many other cultures of black and brown people that speak different languages and have diverse cultures and traditions.

Did you know there is a population of over 50,000 people identified as "African" all the way in Russia?

Did you know that the richest man in all of recorded history was a black man? His name was Mansa Musa and he ruled the Mali Empire, which was located in West Africa. He conquered 24 cities and was a lifelong student and lover of science, literature, the arts and architecture. Talk about coping like a king! There is so much to know about your culture and history. I encourage you to not limit your understanding of your history to slavery and oppression but to have pride in all the beauty and history of your culture.

Do some research; you might find some very interesting and wonderful things about your ancestors that you can take pride in.

WHO ARE YOU?

As you have learned throughout this first section, you are a unique person. You like to do certain things, people see you a certain way and you have emotions that you naturally feel. You are triggered by things and those triggers affect your moods. You also have a spiritual part of you and it is a part of the way you live your life with your family.

Your culture is the specific traditions and customs that you grow up with, the way in which you live your daily life. It is a part of you. There are celebrations and traditions that you take part in that you enjoy or maybe not so much, but they help shape who you are.

In the next section, we will talk about how you are doing. We will look at your current daily feelings, what to do when you are having a hard time, and the people you can talk to that are available to help you.

Rhodes 5 W's of Life

Who	Who you are matters. Don't change your essence.
What	What you do is important. Plan to succeed.
When	When you have an opportunity, take it, and if you don't have one, make one.
Where	Where there is a choice, make the one that will make you proud.
Why	Why things happen is sometimes hard to explain. Talk it, walk it out and keep pushing.

HOW ARE YOU?

"Dear Young Black Males,

It's okay to be different.
Don't be afaid to be yourself.
Have courage!
Follow your dreams,
No matter how BIG your dreams may seem.

Attitude is everything!
Make sure that you keep a positive one,
In spite of any obstacles that may come your way.
Don't be so quick to give up, and please remember
That self-discipline is your friend.

Be strong, persevere, and most importantly,
BELIEVE in yourself.
Don't listen to anybody's negativity.
Move forward knowing that you CAN and you WILL........

Be unstoppable!"

Stephanie Lahart

MELODIE YARBER-RHODES   COPING LIKE A KING

HOW ARE YOU?

So far, you have taken a deeper look into who you are as a person. You have looked at how you see yourself, how other people see you, your emotions, the things you like and dislike, and your cultural and spiritual parts.

Now let's lean into how you are doing and being in this world. What do I mean by this?

When someone asks you "how are you doing", what is a typical response? Usually, it is "fine" or "good". We say those responses out of habit whether we are doing fine or not. Why do you think you say this even when you are having a "not so fine" day?

_____

_____

_____

_____

I often say I am fine or blessed. I say this even when I am not having a good day because I usually only share my true feelings with people who are close to me, like my mother or my husband. And that is okay.

Do you have someone to talk to when you really need to express yourself on bad days?

I hope you do. If not, may I suggest you talk to a friend or school counselor. It is not good to carry around bad feelings all alone.

If you do not want to talk, may I suggest you write it down. Some people find that writing down their feelings and thoughts on paper helps them to feel a lot better.

What works best for you?

Let's come up with a plan to figure out how you are feeling and what method you will use when you are having a not-so-good day.

Right now, I want you to think about how you are feeling. Sit still with your thoughts. What is going on in your mind? Give yourself a minute or two and now write down those thoughts. (please, try to write more than "idk/I don't know")

HOW ARE YOU?

I am thinking...
_____
_____

What are you feeling? Do you feel physical pain in your body? Do you feel sadness? Are you happy? Sit still with your feelings for about two minutes. Now write down what you are feeling

I feel...
_____
_____
_____

Now, why do you think these thoughts and feelings are happening right now? Take a minute to think about it and then write down your thoughts (Again, please, try not to write idk/I don't know)

I am thinking/feeling this because ...
_____
_____
_____

What you have just done is called reflecting on your thoughts and feelings. You are also doing something called analyzing your thoughts and feelings! You didn't know you could do all of that, did you?

I'm proud of you for trying this. If you have done this before, great. If not, I hope it becomes easier for you to do because it can be helpful.

Ok so now, what do we do with all of this information? You can use it to notice when you are good and when things are not going so well. You can use this practice to learn when it is time to ask someone for help.

HOW ARE YOU?

How Are You Doing Today?

Let's start practicing writing how you are feeling. If you have never done this before, it might feel a little weird at first, and that's OK. You might not know what to write. So here are some tips:

- First, think about how your day is going or how it went.
- Recall events or things people said or did and how they made you feel.
- Write down details.
- Be specific. For example: "Today is going just OK. It's only OK because I woke up late and missed my first zoom class. I know that I will miss points because I did not log in on time."

_____

_____

_____

_____

_____

_____

_____

_____

_____

_____

HOW ARE YOU?

Who Do You Talk to When ....

When I was a child and young teen, I found it hard to talk to people; not because I didn't want to, I really didn't like to be around people that I didn't know. I was a listener and an observer; I watched people and things around me more than I spoke. I was more of what people call an "introvert".

Introverts are people who are more comfortable spending time with their own thoughts and feelings. Sometimes they are also called "shy". Introverts do not prefer to be around large crowds or talk too much. That's what I was called for a large portion of my childhood, and as I got older, I did not like being called shy.

I was not shy, I was just very selective about who I wanted around me and even more careful on what I spoke about and who I spoke to. As I got older, that started to change and I became more extroverted. You might find that your personality changes to as you get older, and that is totally fine.

If you are outgoing and full of energy that is cool too. Sometimes, that makes it easier for you to talk to other people when you need help. Either way, I want you to identify at least ONE adult person in your life that you have a good relationship with. I want you to think about that person now and picture them in you mind.

Now write that person's name down and what role they play in your life (for example your mother, or your coach).

_____ my _____

If you have more than one adult person you can talk to, that's great, but I want to make sure you can identify at least one. This is important because there will be times in your life when you will need to talk to an adult you trust. Maybe you have a question about life, or a relationship, whatever it is, you can ask this person. There is a reason why you identified this person and trust this person so just know this person cares about you and it is good to ask them about that thing that is on your mind.

HOW ARE YOU?

As I write this book for you, the entire world is dealing with a pandemic. COVID-19 took over the world in 2020 and affected the way we do things in our country. At the same time, social uprisings began in America after the murder of a man named George Floyd. He was murdered at the hands of the police and all of it was filmed and became international news. So many people have been affected by both these events, and I can bet you might be one of them.

What are your thoughts about the George Floyd incident?
_____
_____

How did it make you feel?_____
_____
_____

Who did you talk to about those feelings, if anyone?_____
_____

What can you do about your feelings?
_____
_____
_____

Are there any other incidents that made you feel angry/sad upset? _____
_____
_____
_____

HOW ARE YOU?

You may have also heard things about immigration and people saying all types of rude things about immigrants coming to the United States. I encourage you to be hopeful about those situations and don't react to rude people.

Maybe you haven't felt that life is hard, and that is OK. If you do, that is OK as well. If you were mad or angry about what you heard or saw on the news, or even what your family members talked about, that is all natural. Your emotions will tell you how you are really feeling and it's up to you to decide what to do what those feelings.

Dealing with a virus, sickness, mean people, racism, and all types of other difficult things can be hard. It can make you sad, mad, anxious, or even numb. Numb means you don't really feel anything at all. Some people automatically become numb to their feelings when it's too much for them to handle or process. Whatever you feel, please know that you can find some way to deal with those feelings in a healthy way and turn those negative things into positive opportunities.

Remember I mentioned earlier that we would talk about how to deal with people who are mean to you? Let's do that now.

If you ever have a day when you feel bad emotionally or mentally, I encourage you to speak to the adult in your life that you trust the most. That could be mom, dad, grandma, grandad, your teacher, or school counselor. I want you to make sure it is an adult.

HOW ARE YOU?

It is cool to have friends and family members your age who share the same thoughts with you, but an adult usually can help you when you are in a tough situation better than someone your age. Adults have access to more resources to help you.

If there is only ONE thing you remember from this book, I want you to remember this - YOU are NOT alone. There are people who really care about you and who love you. They want you to be happy and to succeed. Don't ever give up. Remember your emotions and feelings are temporary and WILL CHANGE. You could be having a really bad day or even a bad week, but believe me, things will get better.

So, when you have a day that is painful, I want you to reach out for help. Sadly, some boys like you feel like they can't talk to anyone or the bad days won't ever stop. Some boys have decided to take their own life because of the pain they feel because they forgot that things can get better. If you ever have a day where you feel like you want to hurt yourself, hurt someone else, or kill yourself, get help immediately.

There is a hotline called the National Suicide Prevention Lifeline and you can call them at 1800-273-TALK (8255) to speak to someone that will help you see through those foggy moments.

There is also a CRISIS hotline text number, you text HOME to 741741 and someone will text you back, 24/7.

It is my hope that you will never feel like this but if you do, please know that you can feel better and there are people who are trained to help you because YOU are that special.

HOW ARE YOU?

What Exactly is a "King"?

And how can you cope like a king?

According to dictionary.com, a king is:

> *"A male sovereign or monarch; a man who holds by life tenure, and usually by hereditary right, the chief authority over a country and people."*

In other words, a king is a leader and his authority over other people is usually inherited-given to him through his blood line.

You are a king because you hold authority over your life. You can control many of the things in your life. Of course there are some exceptions and life circumstances that are out of your control, but you control where you are headed. The choices you make today are preparing you for your future. And one day, you might choose to have a family of your own, and you will hold a leadership position with your wife over your children.

Characteristics of a King:

    A king is a leader.
    A king is responsible.
    A king has integrity.

What are some other characteristics you think of when you hear the word "king?"
_____
_____
_____

History shows that some kings have left a legacy that is positive and something to be proud of, while others are not remembered for good things. Kings rule in different ways using various methods to cope with the responsibilities of their titles.

HOW ARE YOU?

Here are some examples:

King Selassie I - Emperor of Ethiopia (1930-1974), this king's lineage has been said to trace back to King Solomon of the Bible. He is also known as Ras (prince) Tafari. This king is credited with modernizing his country and bringing the region into the League of Nations, the United Nations and forming the Organization of African Unity in 1963.

He prevented further colonization of his country through strong military resistance and used the help of allies to fight off Italian invaders. Eventually, King Selassie I came to be known as a "messiah" to the people of the Rastafarian movement.

King Tut- Tutankhamen was his name and he was only about 9 years old when he assumed the title of Pharaoh. We learned a great deal about Egyptian civilization through what he had in his tomb. It was the most intact tomb ever uncovered. Tons of artifacts, gold and treasure were discovered in his final resting place. He is known worldwide for the riches that were found buried with him.

Henry VIII- although he did things like initiate the English reformation, partly because he wanted to annul his first marriage (get a divorce), he is most widely remembered for his six marriages. In fact, he had a few of his ex-wives beheaded shortly after their marriages were annulled.

He was said to be educated and charismatic, but later on in life became lustful, paranoid and egotistical.

Barack Obama - Although he was not a "king", Barack H. Obama became the first person of African descent to rule the most powerful nation of modern times. His message of hope inspired millions of Americans to vote for him, twice, and his legacy involved the creation of the Affordable Care Act, which provided health care to millions of Americans. He is known as a charismatic, intelligent man who negotiated with others to help all Americans. Some people call him one of the greatest Presidents the United States of America has ever had.

What legacy would you like to leave at the end of your life? Do you want to be known as someone who worked well with others and changed peoples' lives or do you want to be remembered for being egotistical and selfish? The choice is really yours.

HOW ARE YOU COPING?

"You know what is masculine? Masculine is taking care of your mind, your body, and your soul. We take all sorts of pills when we start losing our hair. But what about our mental health?"- Charlamagne Tha God, **Shook One: Anxiety Playing Tricks on Me**

Lennard McKelvy, also known as Charlamagne Tha God is a radio personality and a New York Times best selling author. He promotes spending time talking about your mental health with a professional. He states "I have had anxiety literally my whole life." Charlamagne is consistently vocal about the necessity of "unpacking" the issues he struggles with as he goes to his weekly therapy sessions.

HOW ARE YOUR COPING?

7 Ways to Cope

If you struggle with finding things to help you cope, or deal with things that bother you, here are my top 7 ways to deal with challenges and changes.

1. REMEMBER WHO YOU ARE

Knowing who you are is the first step in coping. You are one of a kind. You are unique. This is where you learn how you can respond to things. Remember, knowing who you are means, knowing you. Remembering who you are in times of stress, or anger will help you cope with those situations.

How do you do this?

- Think about yourself and what is important to you.
- Consider your family, cultural and spiritual beliefs and practices. What does your faith tell you to do during hard and difficult times?
- Try new things to see if you like them or not. Be open to new possibilities so you can continue to discover what works best for you.

HOW ARE YOU COPING?

2. TRY PROGRESSIVE MUSCLE RELAXATION

Progressive muscle relaxation can be used when you are feeling stressed, anxious, or when you want to feel more relaxed.

- Begin by either sitting on a chair with your feet flat on the ground, or sitting in a comfortable position.
- Focus on one part of your body. Start with your hands. Ball your fingers up into a fist, as tight as you can. Hold for 5 seconds, then release. Your hands should feel more relaxed after releasing (if not, increase the squeeze for 7 or 10 seconds).
- Repeat with your face, shoulders, legs, and toes. Finish with all of your muscles at once. Release and you should feel a greater feeling of relaxation.

HOW ARE YOU COPING?

3. EXERCISE.

There is a strong connection between physical activity and good mental health. And the good news is, you don't need to join a gym to exercise.

Here are few examples of exercises you can try when you are feeling depressed, anxious or sluggish:

- Jogging in place. Jog in place for 1 minute intervals. (60 seconds at a time. Stop for 30 seconds, then repeat).
- Walking. Walk for 20-30 minutes outside when the weather permits.
- Walk up and down the stairs. (Did you know they have a stair climbing machine at the gym? You can use any staircase and it's just as good).
- Jump rope. This is a great aerobic exercise (aerobic basically means you increase your oxygen intake and make your cardiovascular system work better).
- Do squats. Squats allow you to work on several different muscle groups in your body at one time. YouTube has several videos on the best way to do properly do squats. Or ask you school physical education teacher to show you.
- Lunges. You can do lunges inside or outside. YouTube has several videos on great lunge form as well.
- Participate in physical education/team sports at school. A lot of my former male students really enjoy participating in school physical activities. If you don't, try to participate and think of how much good you are doing to improve your mental health.

HOW ARE YOU COPING?

4. TALK TO SOMEONE YOU TRUST.

A listening ear can be just what you need to help you cope. I know some of you do not like to talk about your feelings, but you would be amazed by how good you can feel when you let some things off your chest by talking to a friend or loved one.

Talking does two things for you:

1) Talking allows you to express yourself to another human being. This in and of itself can have a calming effect on your body. When we release what's on our minds and in our thoughts, that can actually help us to feel better.

2) Talking to another person is a great way to get feedback or solutions. When we have problems or feel a certain way, you can talk to someone who cares and they will provide you with ideas on how they may have handled the situation. They can also be a reflector, or person who can help you make sense of what you are thinking or feeling.

> **RESEARCH SHOWS THAT LISTENING OR BEING ABLE TO HEAR ANOTHER PERSON'S VOICE IS THE SIGNAL THAT CREATES UNDERSTANDING AND CONNECTION (Harvard Business review, Oct 2020. retrieved March 5, 2021)**

HOW ARE YOU COPING?

Kings and rulers around the world oftentimes have advisors they talk to. Kings need people to talk to just like any other person in the world. Talking about problems and receiving counsel are some of the best things a leader can do in order to maintain his kingdom and his ruler-ship.

Think about how this applies to your life?
_____
_____

Can you think of any reason a king or president might want to talk to advisors?
_____
_____

HOW ARE YOU COPING?

5. WRITE

Writing your thoughts down is very therapeutic and helps many people to feel more relaxed and relieved. Try writing in a journal. You can find one at a store, find one online, or buy a composition book and make one of your won.

Also, try writing a song, rap, essay, or poem. You might feel some relief or even a feeling of accomplishment when you write a creative piece. Keep a book or file on your computer or phone to collect your writings.

> *"Writing is the best way to talk without being interrupted".* Jules Renard

When I was younger, I found that it was easier for me to write when I was upset or feeling bad about something. I also discovered that at that time, I was able to convey my true feelings when I wrote them down instead of trying to talk it out with someone. It would give me the push I needed to get the words out of my head.

One of my favorite writers, Ta-Nehisi Coates once said:

> *"The best part of writing is not the communication of knowledge to other people, but the acquisition and synthesizing of knowledge for oneself".*

Ta-Nehisi Coates is a black man who grew up in Baltimore during a very rough and tough time in that city. In his book Between the World and Me (2015) he wrote about his childhood growing up in the inner city and how he experienced a daily fear of violence. He began writing poetry at the age of 17 and he eventually became a New York Time's best-selling author. He experienced a lot of things that made him question the world around him and he was able to process those things through writing.

Maybe you too will benefit from writing. Give it a try. You never know where it will take you.

I have included space at the end of this book to help you get into the habit of writing down your thoughts. If you find that it makes you feel better, in any way, I encourage you to continue writing and develop your creativity in it.

HOW ARE YOU COPING?

6. LISTEN TO MUSIC

Music can contribute to calmer moods, and feelings of joy. Classical music and soft, upbeat instrumental music have been shown to improve moods.

At the same time music can contribute to feelings of sadness, anger and anxiety. Be careful about your music choices when you are "in your feelings". What do I mean?

If you are experiencing something sad, it is not always a good idea to listen to sad content in a song. This can influence your mood and make you feel even more down or depressed which is not what you need to feel better.

There will be times when you will grieve a loss - of friendship, relationship, relative, routine, or anything else - and that is a part of life. What you do not want to get into the habit of doing is focusing on the sadness, rather, you want to put your energy in finding songs/raps/poems that can inspire you to feel better.

What are some ways music has helped you?_____

_____

Who are your favorite musical artists? _____

_____

HOW ARE YOU COPING?

7. PRAY AND/OR MEDITATE

Prayer and meditation are often associated with each other, but they are very different.

Prayer is used by many religions around the world. Praying helps millions of people feel like they are being heard, and it makes them feel hopeful about the future. For some religions such as Islam, prayer is actually a requirement for those who are practicing the beliefs of that religion; Muslims pray five times a day. Some religions have certain formats for praying while others believe in freely speaking your thoughts to a higher power.

Meditation, on the other hand, is a process of training your mind to focus on one thing, or nothing! It is also used to learn how to re-direct your thoughts. According to the American Psychology Association's definition, meditation is used to "gain insight into oneself and the world", and is "now used to provide relaxation and relief from stress, treat such symptoms as high blood pressure, pain, and insomnia, and promote overall health and well-being." (APA Dictionary of Psychology.https://Dictionary.apa.org/meditation)

There are different types of meditation, and here are some of the most popular examples :

    Mindfulness meditation

    Progressive relaxation meditation (discussed previously)

    Guided imagery relaxation/meditation

WHAT DO YOU NEED TO SUCCEED?

"Some people want it to happen, some wish it would happen, others make it happen."

-Michael Jordan

WHAT DO YOU NEED TO SUCCEED?

The most successful people in life have some of the same things in common. They get up early, set goals, believe in themselves, and never stop trying.

Success also means different things to different people; but when I say what do you need to succeed, I am talking about the things you will need to live a life you are proud of. Success to me is achieving the goals you set for yourself and your life. Success can also mean overcoming challenges in your life to do the best that you can with your life.
What does SUCCESS mean to you?

Hint: Think about FAMILY, CAREER, current GOALS and THINGS YOU WANT IN LIFE
_____

_____

_____

Name some people you see as successful, and explain why you think they are successful:

1._____

Why do I see this person as successful?
_____

2._____

Why do I see this person as successful?
_____

_____

3._____

Why do I see this person as successful?
_____

_____

WHAT DO YOU NEED TO SUCCEED?

MY PICTURE OF SUCCESS

In the box below, draw or paste pictures of things or people you would include in your picture of success.

MELODIE YARBER-RHODES   COPING LIKE A KING

WHAT DO YOU NEED TO SUCCEED?

Planning For Success

You are never too young to start planning for your future. Planning for the future could mean planning for the remainder of the 9 weeks, the next semester or the next school year. I know you probably do not often plan ahead, however, developing that habit can be very beneficial for your success.

Let's review what you put for your picture of success. Hopefully that exercise helped you to think about your future and the goals you have for yourself. If not, let's start now.

A goal is something you hope to accomplish one day. You can have short-term goals (things you want to accomplish in the next 6 months to a year) and long-term goals (things you want to accomplish in the next few years).

Do you have any goals? If so, I want you to write at least 3 here:

1._____

_____

2._____

_____

3._____

_____

"*A dream without a goal is a wish.*"
Antoine de Saint-Exupery
"*A goal without a plan is just a dream.*"
Unknown

WHAT DO YOU NEED TO SUCCEED?

Let's take a look at each goal and develop a plan for that goal. A goal should be S.M.A.R.T. The chart below explains what this means.

SMART GOALS

S	**SPECIFIC**	State exactly what you want to accomplish.
M	**MEASURABLE**	Use smaller, mini goals to measure your progress.
A	**ACHIEVEABLE**	Make your goal reasonable.
R	**REALISTIC**	Set a goal that is relevant to your life.
T	**TIMELY**	Give yourself time but, set a deadline.

If you need more information on your goal, do some research. We all have dreams and goals, but sometimes we get discouraged because we don't know how to do it.

There are people in your school, family, and community who can help you achieve your goals. You can ask them, use google, or even go to your local library to find the answers you seek.

Let's look at each one of your goals to see if they are S.M.A.R.T:

WHAT DO YOU NEED TO SUCCEED?

GOAL 1._____

_____

| Is this goal *specific*? If no, change it. | EXAMPLE: I want to earn straight A's next 9 weeks |

| Can you *measure* the progress of this goal? How long will each step take? | EXAMPLE I will check my grades, turn in all assignments and talk to my teachers every friday to make sure I am on track. |

Is this *achievable* and *reasonable*? (for example, you will not be able to lose 30 lbs in one day)

Is this goal *realistic* and *relevant* to your life and what you want to do?

Is there a *time* set for you to accomplish this goal? When should you be able to achieve this goal?

Re-write your goal the S.M.A.R.T way! _____

_____

MELODIE YARBER-RHODES   COPING LIKE A KING

WHAT DO YOU NEED TO SUCCEED?

GOAL 2._____

Is this goal *specific*? If no, change it.

Can you *measure* the progress of this goal? How long will each step take?

Is this *achievable* and *reasonable*? (for example, you will not be able to lose 30 lbs in one day)

Is this goal *realistic* and *relevant* to your life and what you want to do?

Is there a *time* set for you to accomplish this goal? When should you be able to achieve this goal?

Re-write your goal the S.M.A.R.T way! _____

MELODIE YARBER-RHODES  COPING LIKE A KING

WHAT DO YOU NEED TO SUCCEED?

GOAL 3. _____

Is this goal *specific*? If no, change it.

Can you *measure* the progress of this goal? How long will each step take?

Is this *achievable* and *reasonable*? (for example, you will not be able to lose 30 lbs in one day)

Is this goal *realistic* and *relevant* to your life and what you want to do?

Is there a *time* set for you to accomplish this goal? When should you be able to achieve this goal?

Re-write your goal the S.M.A.R.T way! _____

MELODIE YARBER-RHODES   COPING LIKE A KING

WHAT DO YOU NEED TO SUCCEED?

Skills

> *"Hold fast to dreams, For if dreams die*
> *Life is a broken-winged bird,*
> *That cannot fly."*
>
> Langston Hughes

Along with your goals comes something else that successful people have in common. Great athletes like Michael Jordan and Arthur Ashe, rappers/poets such as Jay-Z and Kendrick Lamar and comedians Kevin Hart, and Steve Harvey did not become "great" overnight. Each one of these people have found success in their field due to a few things, one most important of those is skill.

Skill is simply the ability to do something, and being persistent at that "something" builds skill.

What do I mean? Some people give up on their goals because it takes some type of skill, and skill requires a lot of repetitive learning in order to complete that goal competently. As the Merriam-Webster dictionary defines it, skill is:

> *"A learned power of doing something competently."*

The key words you can focus in on now are "learned" and "power". Some people give up on their goals because it takes some type of skill, and skill takes learning; a lot of learning in order to complete that goal competently.

Don't give up on your dreams and goals because you lack the discipline to keep learning and accepting correction from someone who has been where you want to be. Now is the time to understand this concept and keep striving to practice the skills that will lead you to accomplishing your goals.

WHAT DO YOU NEED TO SUCCEED?

Use the space below to list 3 skills you will work on this year and how you will work on them.

Hint: The skills you list can be related to the S.M.A.R.T goals you previously listed.

Skill 1: _____

_____

How will you practice this skill, and with whom? _____

_____

How often? _____

Skill 2: _____

_____

How will you practice this skill, and with whom ? _____

_____

How often? _____

Skill 3: _____

_____

How will you practice this skill, and with whom ? _____

_____

How often? _____

WHAT DO YOU NEED TO SUCCEED?

"Any time you have an opportunity to make a difference in this world and you don't, then you are wasting your time on earth."

- Roberto Clemente

Roberto Clemente paved the way for Hispanic Americans in Major League Baseball. He was a pioneer of the game. In 1960, Clemente, wearing the iconic number 21, went on to become the first Latin American and Caribbean to win a World Series as a starter.

WHAT DO YOU NEED TO SUCCEED?

Has Anyone Ever Told You...?

There are some things in life that we learn from our parents or other adults that help to make us more prepared and successful in life.

Let's look at some things I learned as a child that I passed on to my son, and now I'm passing on to you. These things helped and still help me feel prepared, lessen anxiety, and keep me focused on my goals.

That equals SUCCESS.

Here are some things that can help you to be successful and achieve your goals:

Routines

Having routines will help you in A LOT of ways. Routines help you to plan your day and know what to expect every day. Routines give you consistency which is very good. Routines also calm you down. One good routine is a bed-time routine.

Sleep

Boys your age need about 9 - 11 hours of sleep each night. Make sure you have a regular bed time, so you can be alert during the day! Your parent/guardian should not have to remind you to get some rest.

WHAT DO YOU NEED TO SUCCEED?

Eat Fruits and Vegetables

Research shows you really are what you eat! Well, you feel what you eat is closer to the truth. According to the research of several neuroimmunologist and other scientists, if you change what's in your gut (stomach), you can change your brain chemistry. The types of food you eat affect the bacteria in your digestive system and in turn, that affects your mood and behavior. There is also a strong link between taking things called pro-biotics and having positive moods.

So, start early… watch what you put inside your gut.

WHAT DO YOU NEED TO SUCCEED?

Exercise

Exercising at least 30 minutes a day is a good start. If you can, tryout for a sport, the band, or some sort of school or community activity that can get you moving.

INSPIRATION

Inspiration

Now that you are at this point in the book, you know more about yourself, you know more about your goals, and you have learned some new ways to cope with hard times. Hopefully, you have been inspired.

INSPIRATION
/in·spi·ra·tion/
the action or power of moving the intellect or emotions

Being "inspired" has many meanings and there are many ways for it to happen, but let's think about ways you can inspire yourself.

I want you to think about at least 3 things you have accomplished in your life. Write them down and describe how you did it, who may have helped you, if anyone, and how you felt when you accomplished it.

Hint: it can be anything from performing in a recital to acing a science test.

My accomplishments:

Accomplishment	Who helped you?	How did you feel?
1)		
2)		
3)		

INSPIRATION

Inspiration can come from an outside source as well.

Who is your hero? Who is the person and or person(s) who have inspired you?

Let's take a minute to really think about this. Many career coaches and life coaches say that certain people inspire you for a reason. This reason is that you make some type of connection with what you see in their life and it could be a sign that whatever they do is something you might want to do in the future.

For example, I have always admired, Oprah Winfrey (I call her Queen Oprah). Every time I read one of her books or watch her interviews, I am inspired by her words and her life story. I realized that one of the things I connected with Oprah was that she loved to teach. Although it wasn't in a classroom, Oprah Winfrey used her daytime talk-show and many other projects to teach others about various topics. She is an educator and I identified with that part of her story. I am an educator at the very core of me, and I find it very fulfilling when I see others doing the same thing.

In the chart below, identify at least 3 people who inspire you, and try your best to figure out exactly why they inspire you and what exactly it is that they do to inspire you.

Hint: Your inspiring figure can be a celebrity, but they do not have to be. It can be someone in your family or community.

Inspiring figure	Why do they inspire you?	What do they do that inspires you?
1)		
2)		
3)		

No matter who you pick and what they do, or do not do, you can always be inspired by YOU! Look at how far you have come in life… and how much further you will go.

"Inspiration exists, but it has to find you working."- Pablo Picasso

CONCLUSION

I wrote this book for you because I believe in you. I wrote this book for you because I know you have seen some things in life that have made you angry, sad, mad, and confused and I want you to be able to process and unpack those things.

I wrote this book for you because I want you to have a resource specifically for you to use and learn more about yourself and your culture.

I wrote this book for you because you are my son too. A future king in this world.

There are so many things that you have accomplished in life already! You should be proud of yourself. You have done so many things right and you have to forgive yourself for anything you have done that you regret doing. Today is a new day for you so use it to push you along.

My hope is that you get to know yourself better as you complete the exercises and return to them as needed and that you are inspired to do great things. My hope is also that you find this helpful in your journey in life and that you can begin coping like the King you are becoming.

30 DAY JOURNAL WRITING CHALLENGE

There are all types of challenges on social media. Most of them are dance-related challenges that can be fun and great for entertainment. Now I want you to try a different kind of challenge.

Now that you know how to write your feelings and thoughts down, I want you to try to write for the next 30 days straight! Remember, you can write thoughts, feelings, sentences or even write like you are speaking to somebody. As I mentioned before, you might struggle to write at first, but after you write for a little while, it will become easier.

(Tip: Try writing at the same time each day to stay consistent)

Get Busy

Day 1

_____

_____

_____

_____

_____

Day 2

_____

_____

_____

Day 3

Day 4

Day 5

Day 6

Day 7

Day 8

Day 9

Day 10

Day 11

Day 12

Day 13

Day 14

Day 15

Day 16

Day 17

Day 18

Day 19

Day 20

Day 21

___

___

___

___

Day 22

___

___

___

___

Day 23

___

___

___

___

Day 24

_____

_____

_____

_____

_____

Day 25

_____

_____

_____

_____

_____

Day 26

_____

_____

_____

_____

_____

Day 27

Day 28

Day 29

Day 30

Congratulations!

You Did A Great Job!

ACKNOWLEDGEMENTS

Thank you to all my "sons" I have met over the years. Thank you for inspiring me throughout my career, and for being brave enough to share your feelings with me.

I would also like to thank the sons I gave birth to. You are my main inspiration and power source for fighting for the things I believe in.

Thank you to my husband for having patience with me.

Thank you to everyone who helped me complete this work.

ABOUT THE AUTHOR

Melodie Yarber-Rhodes

Melodie Yarber-Rhodes is a career therapist and counselor. She has been an educator and counselor for over 17 years. Melodie has worked with students from all ages and from all walks of life.

During her tenure as the Mental Health Coordinator & Facilitator for the Mindful Schools Program (Polk County Public Schools) she helped to promote mental health awareness and led a campaign to increase student involvement in improving their mental health. Melodie also became a certified Youth Mental Health First Aid (YMHFA) instructor. Through the YMHFA program, she teaches principals, counselors, and other school staff to recognize the symptoms of distressed students to get them the help they desperately need.

Mrs. Yarber-Rhodes attended The Florida State University where she received her bachelor's degree in psychology and then went on to earn her Master of Arts degree in community counseling. She has had extensive training in Trauma-Informed Care, Cognitive Behavioral Therapy, and Solution-Focused Brief Therapy.

Melodie enjoys writing, listening to all genres of music, social media surfing, volunteering and helping others in every way that she can. She is married to Mr. Tarrence Rhodes, and has two beautiful, energetic boys, Micaiah 16, Mason 2 years old, and an even more energetic, silver poodle named Prince Akeem.